# WHY SETTLE FOR A SLICE, WHEN YOU CAN HAVE THE WHOLE PIE!

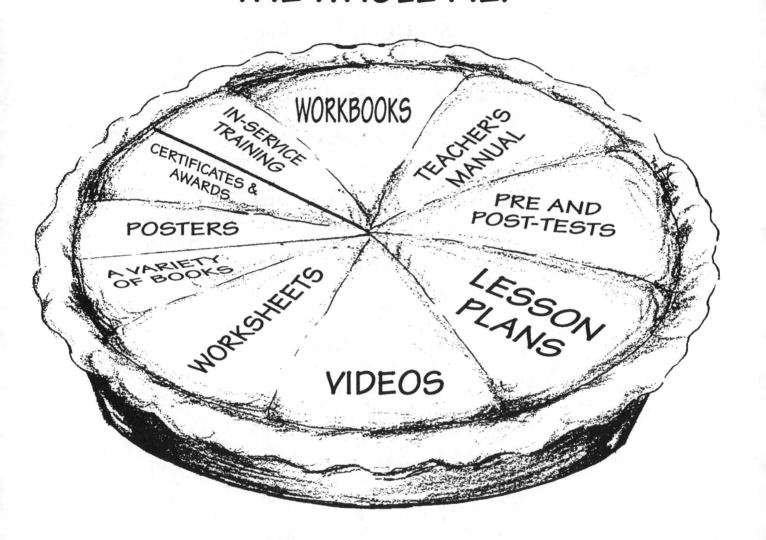

The workbooks are designed for K-12 and are a very important component of SETCLAE's comprehensive, Africentric, multicultural curriculum.

# SETCLAE

## Self-Esteem Through Culture Leads to Academic Excellence

## 6th Grade Workbook

Harambee Session Illustrations by Reginald Mackey
First Edition, Second Printing
Copyright 1992 by Doriel R. Mackay, M.A. and Jawanza Kunjufu, Ph.D.

*Kiswahili for Dependable & Cheerful*

*Visit our web site at*
**http://**
**www.AfricanAmericanImages.com**
*or*
*e-mail us at*
**AAI@AfricanAmericanImages.com**

# African American Images
# Chicago, Illinois

# ACKNOWLEDGMENTS

*I would like to thank the following individuals for their contributions in making this workbook possible:*

*Dr. Jawanza Kunjufu and Folami Prescott,*
*for their vision in creating this model curriculum for our youth.*

*Ms. Rita Smith-Kunjufu,*
*for her clear directions and serenity.*

*Dr. Gwendolyn Brooks,*
*my distinguished Professor of English at Chicago State University,*
*for holding the torch high and lighting my way.*

*Haki Madhubuti,*
*my esteemed Professor of English at Chicago State University,*
*for being an excellent teacher.*

*Dr. Margaret Duggar,*
*Professor of English at Chicago State University for sharing*
*her knowledge and humor during my studies.*

*Ms. Kimberly Vann,*
*African American Images, for her coordinating efforts and patience.*

*Ms. Adrian Payton-Williams,*
*African American Images, for her technical support.*

*Ms. Charlene Snelling,*
*Resource Librarian, Chicago State University for her encouragement and finally,*
*the Creator of the Universe without whom nothing would exist.*

*Doriel R. Mackay, M.A.*

# THE SETCLAE WORKBOOK
# SIXTH GRADE

# TABLE OF CONTENTS

# INTRODUCTION

Jambo mwanafunzi (Hello students)! Welcome to SETCLAE! This program was designed to help you achieve excellence in your studies in school by making you aware of your history and goals to strive towards. SETCLAE should also help you achieve self-esteem and develop love for your family, friends, classmates and communities. You will address the meaning of your favorite songs, relationships with your friends and family, your feelings about school, what it means to be a man or woman, and some very important, enlightening lessons regarding African and African American history and culture.

Our concern for you will become very clear as you continue to use this workbook. It offers a great deal of activities, exercises, and ideas for you to use and share with others. In fact, working with others is the name of the game in SETCLAE. Working in Harambee Groups (Harambee means "Let's Pull Together" in Kiswahili), you, your peers and family members (extended and otherwise) will learn, sing, dance, learn, act, write, learn, discuss, think, and grow as you explore some of the most critical issues concerning and affecting our families and communities. For each Harambee Time, there are a number of activities. The Harambee Group symbol (HG), which is adjacent to the word Materials, lets you know you will be working with your Harambee Group for that session.

We teachers (mwalimu) hope that as we try to impart this knowledge to you and share some basic principles with each other that we both shall grow. These principles are:

Umoja - Unity
Ujima - Collective work and responsibility
Kujichagulia - Self-determination
Ujamaa - Cooperative Economics
Nia - Purpose
Kuumba - Creativity
Imani - Faith

So, HARAMBEE (Let's Pull Together) and let your KUUMBA (Creativity) flow! ! !

# How to Make the Most of Your SETCLAE Journey

In order to get the full benefit from this workbook, you will need to use some additional books as well as participate in some activities and exercises.

**The books you will need on this Journey are:**
*Ashanti to Zulu* by Margaret Musgrove
*Abdul and the Designer Tennis Shoes* by William McDaniels
*I'm Special, Too* by Darlene M. McCurty
*Jomo: A Name to be Proud* by Sharon N. Carter
*Lessons From History* (Jr./Sr.) by Jawanza Kunjufu
*Shining Legacy* by Nkechi Taifa
*Coming of Age: African American Male Rites of Passage* by Paul Hill, Jr.
*Herstory: Black Female Rites of Passage* by Mary Lewis
*Great Negroes Past and Present* by Russell Adams

**Here are a few suggestions that will help you master this material:**
1. Look over the vocabulary list of Kiswahili words. Kiswahili is the language chosen by the Pan-African Congress in 1974 to be an international language amongst peoples of African origin all around the world.

2. Use a variety of materials for your artwork such as: markers, pencils, crayons, paint.

3. Look at magazines like *Ebony, Essence, Jet, YSB, The Source, Emerge, African Commentary, Black Enterprise* and any other material that discusses African and African American people. They are filled with relevant information, lessons from history, and illustrations of Black life.

4. Use your ideas to create poems, raps, skits, songs, dances, dramatic presentations, speeches, plays, books, articles, and letters to share your insight with others.

5. Take your Journal entries seriously. They may be the raw materials for your best-selling autobiography.

6. Use the illustrations of each Harambee Time for bulletin boards, posters and other visual displays.

7. When working in Harambee groups, encourage members to take on tasks according to talents and interests. Each group should identify someone to fulfill the following roles:
   Moderator          Illustrator          Timekeeper          Rapper/Poet
   Reporter           Observer             Recorder

   Of course, one person can perform several of these roles simultaneously.

8. Let your Kuumba (creativity) flow as you create your own poetry, dramatic presentations, and speeches.

9. Share your newfound knowledge with your family and friends.

10. Always remember: everyone is a "mwalimu mwanafunzi" (teacher and student).

11. Never forget what SETCLAE stands for: Self-Esteem Through Culture Leads to Academic Excellence!!!

So now, let's put on our critical thinking caps and begin.

# Correlation of SETCLAE Lessons
# to Academic Objectives

In an effort to accommodate the implementation of SETCLAE into the existing curriculum in your school, the Harambee Time sessions have been correlated to the most common academic objectives for this grade level. The Typical Course of Study for kindergarten through twelfth grade was compiled by World Book Educational Products. Curriculum materials such as the *Nault-Caswell-Brain Analysis of Courses of Study* and others from The National Council of Teachers of Mathematics, English, and Social Studies were analyzed in the preparation of the study guide.

Please use this guide to help give SETCLAE a home in your setting. You will soon see that the program is a welcome and valuable member of the family. The HARAMBEE TIME can be effective in "pulling us together" as we build Tomorrow's Leaders. We also encourage you to incorporate the learning and classroom management styles (e.g. student-made materials and Harambee groups respectively) used in SETCLAE into all subjects taught. And share your success stories with your colleagues!

SS -- Social Studies / LA -- Language Arts / HT -- Health / MT -- Mathematics

**1 ---- Let Me Introduce Myself**
  LA   Note taking skills
       Report writing skills

**2 ---- Bonding**
  LA   Note taking skills
       Research skills
       Listening and speech activities
       Collective decision making

**3 ---- Rules, Rights, and Responsibilities**
  LA   Deductive reasoning

**4 ---- Positive People Praising**
  LA   Report writing skills
       Listening/spelling skills

**5 ---- Goal Setting**
  LA   Deductive reasoning

**6 ---- Careers - I Can Be!**
  LA   Report writing skills
       Listening and speech activities

**7 ----- Me and My Family**
  LA   Literal and Inferential reading skills
       Writing skills

**8 ----- Names We Call Ourselves**
  LA   Extended vocabulary
       Literal and Inferential reading skills

**9 ----- The Color Question**
  LA   Writing skills
       Listening and speech activities

**10 -- *Lessons* Video
     with Dr. Jawanza Kunjufu**
  LA   Critique
  SS   Our American culture
  HT   Type and functions of food
       Body's utilization of food

**11 --- Africa, The Continent**
  SS   Map and globe skills
       Our Native background
       Exploration and discovery
  LA   Writing skills

# SETCLAE Vocabulary Means WORD POWER!!

There is a great deal of power in having a large vocabulary. With a greater understanding of more words, there comes a greater understanding of the world around us and an ability to express what we see, think, and attempt to comprehend. Use the words listed below that are introduced in the Harambee Times noted. Use them in your home, school, among friends and others. Just watch for the power!

**Harambee Time 6**
enunciate

**Harambee Time 8**
descriptive
complimentary
derogatory

**Harambee Time 9**
continent
minority

**Harambee Time 11**
immunization
passport

**Harambee Time 12**
ankh
valley
pyramid
scarab
scepter

**Harambee Time 13**
diaspora

**Harambee Time 19**
dialect
media

**Harambee Time 20**
campaign
ensure

**Harambee Time 23**
commercial
product

**Harambee Time 24**
values

**Harambee Time 25**
advertising
influence

**Harambee Time 29**
principle

**Harambee Time 30**
benefit
inherit

**Harambee Time 31**
economics

**Harambee Time 32**
moderator

# The SETCLAE Student Profile

## 6th Grade

## Instructions

Please answer the following questions on the answer sheet and think very hard about how you feel before answering each one. THERE ARE NO RIGHT OR WRONG ANSWERS. We want YOUR answers.

## Part I

Read each statement or question. If it is true for you, circle "a" on the answer sheet. If it is not true for you, circle "b". Answer every question, even if it's hard to decide. (Just think about yourself and what's important to you.) Select only one answer for each question.

| | | | |
|---|---|---|---|
| 1. | I like to be alone sometimes. | a. Yes | b. No |
| 2. | I enjoy public speaking. | a. Yes | b. No |
| 3. | Cleaning up should be done collectively. | a. Yes | b. No |
| 4. | School will help me to accomplish my own goals. | a. Yes | b. No |
| 5. | I enjoy looking for positive things to say about people. | a. Yes | b. No |
| 6. | I have personal goals. | a. Yes | b. No |
| 7. | I would rather do an extra credit project by myself than with a small group. | a. Yes | b. No |
| 8. | I get upset when things don't go my way. | a. Yes | b. No |
| 9. | School is boring most of the time. | a. Yes | b. No |
| 10. | I speak more than one dialect. | a. Yes | b. No |
| 11. | If I don't see a trash can, I throw my trash on the ground. | a. Yes | b. No |
| 12. | I like participating in special projects like science fairs and spelling bees. | a. Yes | b. No |
| 13. | When the truth is hard to say, I don't say it. | a. Yes | b. No |
| 14. | My friends are more important to me than my family. | a. Yes | b. No |
| 15. | My neighborhood is a good place to live in. | a. Yes | b. No |
| 16. | I can get any job I want, if I work at it hard enough. | a. Yes | b. No |
| 17. | I like being with people that are different from me. | a. Yes | b. No |
| 18. | I like me! | a. Yes | b. No |

| | | | | |
|---|---|---|---|---|
| 19. | Do you believe you can have your own business when you get older? | a. Yes | b. No |
| 20. | The contribution I make to the world is not as important as the contributions of more famous people. | a. Yes | b. No |
| 21. | African Americans have not made many achievements in math, science, technology, and business. | a. Yes | b. No |
| 22. | If I could, I would make friends with people of all races. | a. Yes | b. No |
| 23. | Black people are not able to compete with others in many areas. | a. Yes | b. No |
| 24. | I want to be able to speak Standard English in certain situations. | a. Yes | b. No |

## Part II

Read each item carefully. If it is something that is important to you, circle "a" on the answer sheet. If it is not important to you (it doesn't really matter or has nothing to do with you), circle "b". Take your time and think about it. THERE ARE NO RIGHT OR WRONG ANSWERS. We want to know YOUR FEELINGS.

1. Helping others — a. Important to me — b. Not important to me

2. What others think of me — a. Important to me — b. Not important to me

3. Reading in a study group — a. Important to me — b. Not important to me

4. Television as a way to receive most of my information — a. Important to me — b. Not important to me

5. Solving problems by fighting — a. Important to me — b. Not important to me

6. Learning about my family members - dead and living — a. Important to me — b. Not important to me

7. Working with others on short and long-term projects — a. Important to me — b. Not important to me

8. Doing whatever my friends do — a. Important to me — b. Not important to me

9. Wearing expensive clothes — a. Important to me — b. Not important to me

10. Doing well in school — a. Important to me — b. Not important to me

11. Speaking up for myself and my ideas — a. Important to me — b. Not important to me

12. Being positive most of the time — a. Important to me — b. Not important to me

13. Living conditions in Africa — a. Important to me — b. Not important to me

## Part III

Read each statement carefully. Read the choices. Then select:

"a" if the statement accurately describes you and your feelings.

"b" if the statement does not accurately describe you and your feelings.

Circle them on the answer sheet.

If asked to describe my personality to someone I'd never met, I would use words like:

| | | | |
|---|---|---|---|
| 1. | a leader | a. Yes | b. No |
| 2. | confident | a. Yes | b. No |
| 3. | mature | a. Yes | b. No |
| 4. | critical of others | a. Yes | b. No |
| 5. | proud of my culture | a. Yes | b. No |
| 6. | easily bored | a. Yes | b. No |
| 7. | Africa is a dark continent filled with hunger, poverty and ignorance. | a. True | b. False |
| 8. | I can list five living African American men that are doing positive things in their family, business, church, community, or some other organization. | a. Yes | b. No |

List them below.

1) _____

2) _____

3) _____

4) _____

5) _____

9. Select the one that is most important to you. Choose only one!

a. being popular          b. doing well in school

**Part IV**

Read the following statements and choices for answers carefully. Then pick the answer that most accurately describes your feelings. Circle the letter in front of your answer on the answer sheet.

There are NO RIGHT OR WRONG ANSWERS. Choose the answer that is right for YOU.

1. When my friends have fun without me, I
   a. am happy that they are having fun.
   b. don't even think about it.
   c. wish they weren't having fun without me.

2. When I hear something negative about a person, I
   a. can't wait to tell someone else.
   b. talk to the person to see how I can help.
   c. try to find out more, because it's interesting.

3. When someone says something about me that is not good but is true, I
   a. get upset.
   b. don't want to be around them anymore.
   c. listen and learn from their observations.

4. When someone makes fun of me,
   a. I get upset.
   b. I am hurt.
   c. I laugh with them.
   d. I make a joke of it.
   e. I don't like it.

5. When I am talking to someone, most of the time I look
   a. at their hands.
   b. into their eyes.
   c. at the floor.
   d. all around.

6. I always make sure I am neat and clean in my appearance.
   a. never
   b. once in a while
   c. most of the time

7. Money is important for
   a. buying expensive clothes.
   b. building the community in which we live.
   c. buying whatever I want.
   d. saving for future plans.

8. A girl becomes a woman when (select the answer that is most important to you)
   a. she has a baby.
   b. her body becomes more developed (she has breasts and hair under her arms).
   c. she takes care of herself and her family.
   d. she can talk back to her mother.
   e. she has a boyfriend.

9. When I do poorly on my schoolwork, I
   a. don't really care.
   b. know I tried my best.
   c. know I should try harder.
   d. know it's only because I can't do any better.
   e. know the teacher gave us work that was too hard or boring.

10. In my involvement with organizations, I
    a. like to hold a leadership position.
    b. like to work as a team.
    c. don't like doing the dirty work.
    d. often disagree with other members.

11. When I need help, I
    a. get frustrated.
    b. ask for it.
    c. try to figure it out myself.

12. I pick my friends because
    a. they look good.
    b. they are cool.
    c. they are understanding.
    d. they have something to offer me.

13. I am glad I am the race I am.
    a. Yes
    b. No

14. I chose the answer above because
    a. I am proud of my heritage.
    b. I should be glad.
    c. I study my history and culture.
    d. my friends say it's important.

15. I like my favorite music because
    a. of its rhythm for dancing.
    b. of its positive messages.
    c. of its ability to help me relax.
    d. the rappers curse and insult women.
    e. the videos are nice.

16. A boy becomes a man when
    a. he can handle drugs and crime.
    b. he makes a baby.
    c. he takes responsibility for his actions.
    d. he can fight well.

17. When I attend assemblies or special events, I like to sit
    a. in the middle of the auditorium.
    b. in the front of the auditorium.
    c. in the back of the auditorium.

18. When I set a goal, I
    a. expect someone to make it happen for me.
    b. plan how I will do it and make the first step.
    c. just think about it very hard.
    d. ask my friends to get me started.

19. When the teacher leaves the room, I
    a. talk.
    b. stop doing my work.
    c. look at who is being disobedient.
    d. find something quiet to do once I finish my work.

20. Learning about one's culture and heritage is very important and helps me feel good about who I am.
    a. Yes
    b. No

21. I like my favorite television program because
    a. it's very funny.
    b. I enjoy the action.
    c. I enjoy the "scenery" (cars, clothes, houses, etc.).
    d. it is educational.
    e. it makes me think and discuss important issues with others.

22. I am beautiful or handsome because I have
    a. light skin.
    b. dark skin.
    c. natural hair.
    d. long hair.
    e. a thin shape.

23. Answering these questions was
    a. very enjoyable.
    b. no big deal.
    c. a good way to take a closer look at my personal development.

24. Africa has many cities.
    a. True          b. False

25. Africa is the Motherland of Black people all over the world.
    a. True          b. False

26. Egypt, also known as Kemet (which means Land of the Blacks), is in Africa which is the cradle of civilization.
    a. True          b. False

27. African people have always resisted domination all over the world.
    a. True          b. False

28. Africa is mostly jungle.
    a. True          b. False

29. Tarzan movies show you what Africa is like and used to be like.
    a. True          b. False

30. Africa is a continent on which there is a cultural unity more important than the differences we hear about in the news.
    a. True          b. False

Using the definitions on the right, choose the letter that you feel best describes each of the seven principles listed (Nguzo Saba).

__ 31. UMOJA          a. to build our stores and businesses and profit from them together.

__ 32. KUJICHAGULIA    b. to have a collective goal of building and developing our community.

__ 33. UJIMA          c. to always be creative in the ways we improve our communities.

__ 34. UJAMAA        d. being determined to speak up for ourselves.

__ 35. NIA             e. to work on challenges together and feel responsible as a group.

__ 36. KUUMBA       f. to believe in ourselves that we will do great things.

__ 37. IMANI          g. to keep in touch with and offer support to friends, neighbors, and community.

**Materials:**
🖊 Pen
🖊 Index Cards

**Procedure:**
Using the following Swahili words, tell something about yourself and your family.

Mama-Mother
Baba-Father
Ndada-Sister
Ndugu-Brother

List 10 qualities (adjectives) that best describe how you are or would like to be.

Draw a picture of yourself within the mirror.

NOTES:

_____

_____

_____

_____

_____

**The Journal:**
In your journal, write a brief bio on yourself that could be used to introduce you to an audience. Include your strengths and weaknesses.

# 10 Of My Great Attributes

1 _____

2 _____

3 _____

4 _____

5 _____

6 _____

7 _____

8 _____

9 _____

10 _____

**Postscript...**
Using index cards, make ID cards to include your name, birthplace, favorite TV show, movie and someone you admire.

## Materials: (HG)
- Picture of yourself for ID card
- Pen
- Coloring Materials
- Poster Board

## Procedure:
Your teacher will assign you to a Harambee Group. Working in your Harambee Group, select a name for the group from the choices given.

Group #1-Umoja, Kujichagulia, Ujima, Ujamaa, Nia, Kuumba, Imani

Group #2-Nigeria, Kenya, Egypt, Azania, Tanzania

Group #3-Ashanti, Chagga, Yoruba, Zulu, Pondo

Group #4-Morehouse, Hampton, Spelman, Tuskegee, Howard

Group #5-Scientists, Lawyers, Artists, Educators, Farmers

(For more information on Groups #2, #3, and #4 read "SOMETHING YOU SHOULD KNOW").

Draw a picture of your family engaged in one of the activities that you do together. Try to come up with something besides watching TV together.

## The Journal:
In your journal, write about some activities that you would like to share with your family or classmates.

## Postscript:
Discuss some places and situations where people work together.

## Materials:
✐ Pen

## Procedure:
List some rules, rights, and responsibilities that you have to follow. Place a check mark in the column that best describes how you feel about each item on your list.

NOTES:

_____

_____

_____

_____

_____

_____

_____

_____

_____

_____

_____

_____

_____

_____

_____

# Rules, Rights and Responsibilities

| | Like | Dislike |
|---|---|---|
| **RULES:** | | |
| DO NOT SHOUT IN CLASS | | |
| | | |
| | | |
| | | |
| | | |
| **RIGHTS:** | | |
| I HAVE A RIGHT TO BE TREATED FAIRLY | | |
| | | |
| | | |
| | | |
| | | |
| **RESPONSIBILITIES:** | | |
| KEEPING MY BEDROOM CLEAN | | |
| | | |
| | | |
| | | |

## The Journal:
List your impressions about rules.

## Postscript...
Write a list of rules and rights you want respected.

## Materials:

- *Lessons From History*
- *Poster Boards,
  Markers or Other
  Coloring Materials*
- *Yarn*
- *Glitter*
- *Paint*

## Procedure:

Make a drawing of someone
you most admire in *Lessons
From History* and write a
paragraph about why they're
your favorite person.

NOTES:

_____

_____

_____

_____

_____

_____

_____

_____

_____

_____

## The Journal:

In your journal, write about
someone you like. Also, write
down what you like about
yourself and why.

_____

_____

_____

_____

_____

_____

_____

## Postscript...

Do a skit about the life of a famous person telling his or her story.

**Materials:**
✏ Pen

**Procedure:**
The purpose of this lesson is to help you realize the importance of setting goals. Whatever you want to achieve in life can be accomplished once you determine your talents and interests and determine what steps you need to take. Careful thought and planning are necessary when setting a goal. Follow the steps outlined, so you can see how easy it is to reach any goal you set for yourself.

NOTES:

_____

_____

_____

_____

_____

_____

_____

_____

# Goal Setting

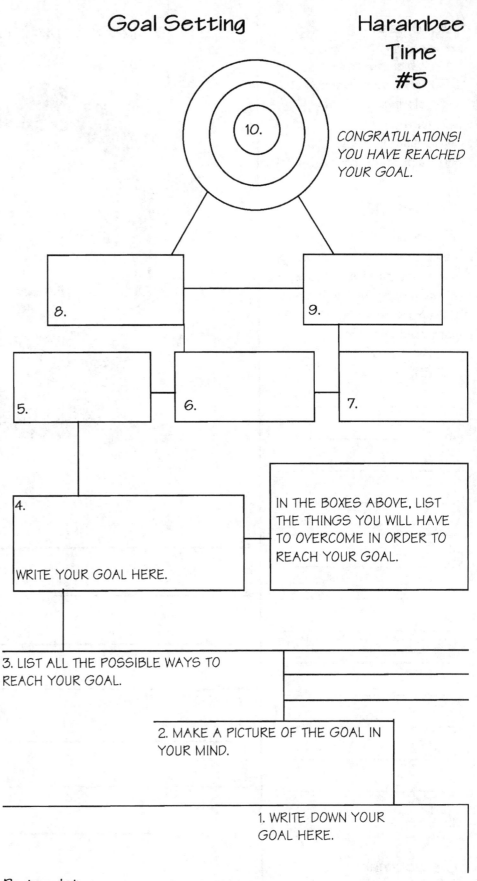

10.

CONGRATULATIONS! YOU HAVE REACHED YOUR GOAL.

8.

9.

5.

6.

7.

4.

WRITE YOUR GOAL HERE.

IN THE BOXES ABOVE, LIST THE THINGS YOU WILL HAVE TO OVERCOME IN ORDER TO REACH YOUR GOAL.

3. LIST ALL THE POSSIBLE WAYS TO REACH YOUR GOAL.

2. MAKE A PICTURE OF THE GOAL IN YOUR MIND.

1. WRITE DOWN YOUR GOAL HERE.

**The Journal:**
List some of the things that you would like to achieve in life within the next 5 years.

**Postscript...**
Interview someone who has achieved a goal which is similar to yours. Find out what steps he or she took to reach the goal. Compare their goal setting plans with your own.

## Materials:
- *Lessons From History*, Chap. 5
- Guest speaker
- Speech on your career choice

## Procedure:
Vote on the kind of person that you would like to come and speak to your class about his or her career. Prepare a two-minute speech on your career choice. Be sure to enunciate your words properly.

NOTES:

_____

_____

_____

_____

_____

_____

_____

_____

_____

_____

## The Journal:
In your journal, pretend you are an adult and write a story about your day at work.

## Postscript...
From *Lessons*, Chapter 5, discuss why these outstanding achievers were important and share their accomplishments with your family members.

## Materials:

- ✐ Marker
- ✐ Construction paper
- ✐ Felt
- ✐ *I'm Special, Too*
- ✐ Glue

## Procedure:

Fill in the tree with the names of your family members. Next, using construction paper, make a tree and use felt for the leaves. Write in the names of your family members and display them, by gluing the leaves on the tree.

NOTES:

_____

_____

_____

_____

_____

_____

_____

_____

_____

_____

_____

## The Journal:

Write something you think is very special about your family.

## Postscript...

After reading the book, discuss the family in *I'm Special, Too*. Are they very different from your family? Explain any differences and/or similarities.

**Materials: (HG)**
- Lessons From History, p. 93-95 (poem)
- Jomo, p. 31-32

## Procedure:

Read the poem written by Margaret Burroughs and see how many descriptive names for people the author has used. List the names that are complimentary and the names that are derogatory in meaning. Practice saying foreign names by reading aloud the list of names in Jomo.

NOTES:

_____

_____

_____

_____

_____

_____

_____

_____

_____

_____

## The Journal:

Think about how you feel when people call you names. Should you do this to others?

DESCRIPTIVE TERMS FROM THE POEM "WHAT SHOULD I TELL MY CHILDREN WHO ARE BLACK?"

| COMPLIMENTARY | DEROGATORY |
|---|---|
|  |  |
|  |  |
|  |  |
|  |  |
|  |  |
|  |  |
|  |  |
|  |  |

WHY DO PEOPLE MAKE FUN OF OTHER PEOPLE?

_____

_____

_____

_____

_____

## Postscript...

Have a day in class when you dress up in native African styles.

**Materials:**
- ✐ Scissors
- ✐ Magazines

**Procedure:**
Look through magazines and cut out pictures of as many different races as you can and tell what continent they came from.

NOTES:

_____

_____

_____

_____

_____

_____

_____

_____

_____

_____

_____

_____

_____

_____

**The Journal:**
Write how you sometimes feel as a minority in America.

## The Color Question

**Postscript...**
Interview someone who belongs to a different racial group. Compare his or her ideas and experiences to yours. Are there any similarities or differences? Explain them.

## Materials: (HG)
- Lessons video
- Television and VCR
- Poster Boards
- Markers

## Procedure:
Watch the *Lessons* video and take notes. Discuss the following questions with your Harambee Group:
1. On what would you spend one million dollars?
2. Would it help your family, your community, or only yourself?
3. What are your talents?
4. How can you improve your talents?
5. Why does Kathy have a boyfriend?
6. What foods do you usually eat everyday?
7. Are they good for you or do they simply taste good?
8. Why should you know your history?

NOTES:

_____

_____

_____

_____

_____

_____

## The Journal:
Write a letter to Dr. Kunjufu that tells him what you thought of the video and what lessons you learned from history.

# Lessons Video with Dr. Jawanza Kunjufu

How did the Rodney King incident affect you? What historical impact will the beating, verdict, and rebellion have on the lives of African Americans?

## Postscript...
As a class, write a letter to the editor of a major newspaper protesting an event you are unhappy about and would like to see changed. Design posters to express your protest. Use catchy slogans and phrases.

## Materials:
- Ashanti to Zulu
- Lessons From History
- Pen
- Map

## Procedure:
Read Chapter 1, Africa, the Beginning of Civilization. Fill in the names of the countries on the African continent. Can you figure out where some of the tribes live?

1. Draw a mountain and label it Mt. Kilimanjaro.

2. Draw a waterfall and label it Victoria Falls. List the country it is in.

NOTES:

_____

_____

_____

_____

_____

_____

_____

_____

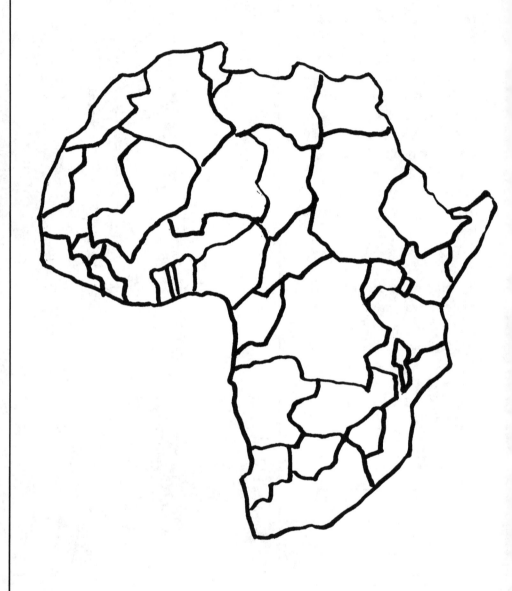

## The Journal:
Write an essay about the outstanding accomplishments Africans made at the beginning of history.

## Postscript...
Plan a trip to Africa. What country will you visit? Call an airline to find out how much it will cost to get there. Will you need any immunization shots? A passport?

## Materials:
- Bus
- Lunch
- *Lessons From History,* Chapter 1

## Procedure:
Visit a museum that exhibits ancient Egyptian artifacts. What is:

a mummy?

a scarab?

a scepter?

an ankh?

Where is the "Valley of the Kings?"

What do African Americans and Egyptians have in common?

NOTES:

_____

_____

_____

_____

_____

_____

_____

_____

_____

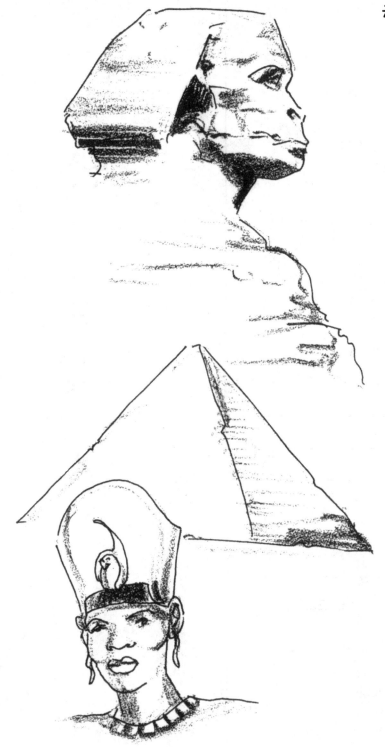

## The Journal:
In your journal, record your impressions of your field trip today.

## Postscript...
Read *Lessons,* Chapter 1 (Africa, the Beginning of Civilization). Have a brainstorming session on how they must have built the pyramids. How did they cut into the stones and lift them into place?

## Materials:
- Toothpicks
- Glue
- Watercolors
- Paper
- *Lessons From History,* p. 86

## Procedure:
After reading *Lessons From History,* draw your own map and label the continents and the ocean in between them. Which ocean is it? Draw a ship or use toothpicks to simulate the ships Africans were transported on.

NOTES:

_____
_____
_____
_____
_____
_____
_____

## The Journal:
Write what it would be like to have lived in Africa a long time ago. Feel free to use your imagination. Also, refer to other chapters in *Lessons From History* and any other African American History books you can locate.

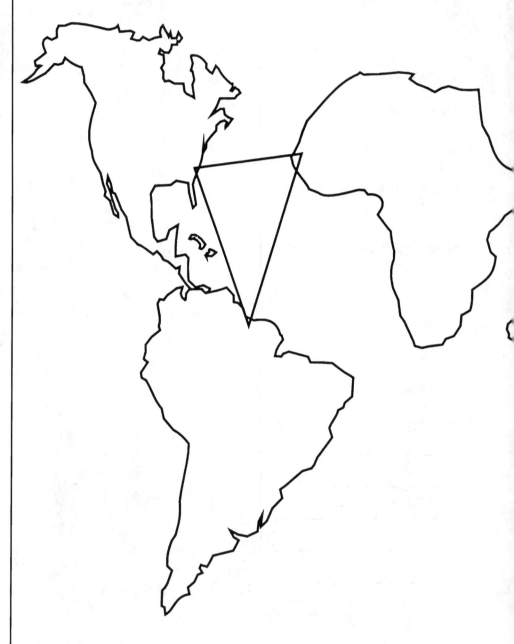

## Postscript...
Discuss how the diaspora has affected African Americans.

## Materials:
- *Shining Legacy, pp 18-22*
- A song "Go Down Moses"

## Procedure:
Read the pages from *Shining Legacy*, then discuss the lives of Harriet Tubman, Sojourner Truth, and Marcus Garvey. Learn the words and the melody to "Go Down Moses."

NOTES:

_____

_____

_____

_____

_____

_____

_____

_____

_____

_____

_____

_____

_____

## The Journal:
Write down how it must have felt to be a runaway slave.

## Postscript...
Discuss the slave codes in America that were oppressive.

## Materials: (HG)

- Poem
- Skit

## Procedure:

Your Harambee Group should perform the skit and recite the poem about Rosa Parks from *Shining Legacy.*

NOTES:

_______________________________

_______________________________

_______________________________

_______________________________

_______________________________

_______________________________

_______________________________

_______________________________

_______________________________

_______________________________

_______________________________

_______________________________

_______________________________

_______________________________

_______________________________

_______________________________

_______________________________

_______________________________

## The Journal:

Record how you enjoyed the skit about Rosa Parks.

# Sitting in the Front

## Harambee Time #15

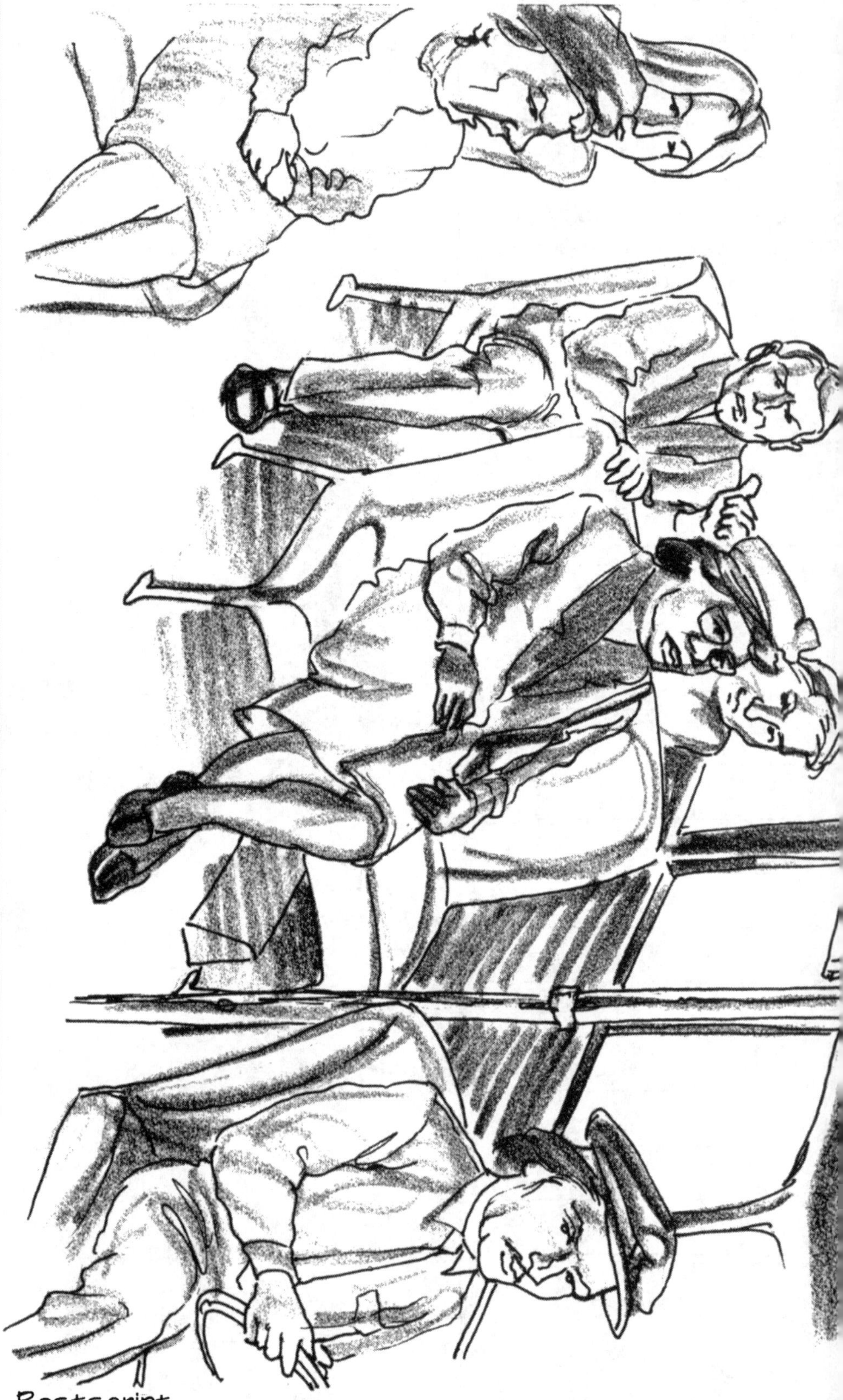

## Postscript...

What emotions do you believe Rosa Parks felt that prompted her actions?

**Materials:**
✏ *Shining Legacy*, p. 2-7

**Procedure:**
Read this poem and discuss it.

What does the elder warn the young boy about?

How were African people stolen away?

What did the brave young brother see?

Who was the African queen that led an army against invaders?

What was the prophecy?

What lesson should have been learned?

What does the word diaspora mean?

Use the word in a sentence.

NOTES:

_____

_____

_____

_____

_____

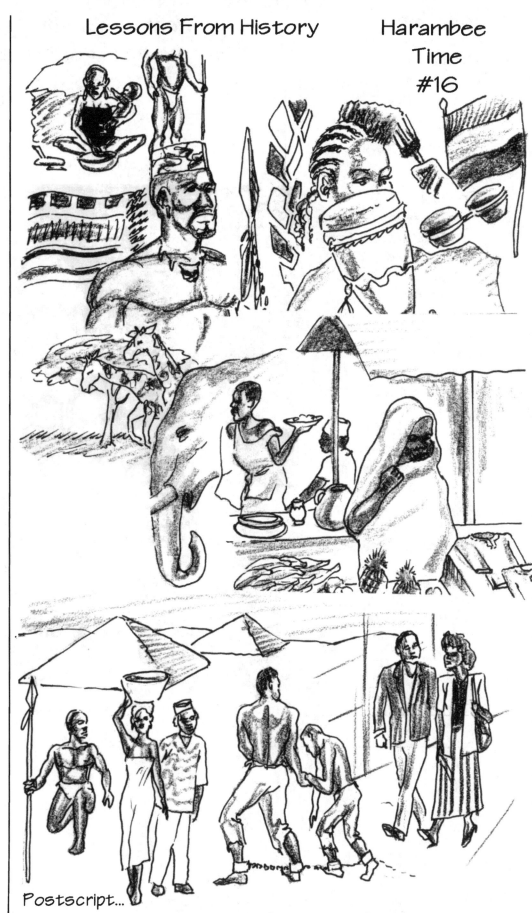

Lessons From History

**The Journal:**
Write how studying history helps us to learn from our mistakes. Give three examples.

**Postscript...**
Use what you have learned and think of ways you can be nicer to your family and friends.

## Materials:
- ✏ *Great Negroes*
- ✏ Scissors
- ✏ Magazines
- ✏ Poster Boards
- ✏ Glue or Tape
- ✏ Index Cards

# African American Excellence and Leadership

## Procedure:
The teacher should create a list of names taken from *Great Negroes'* Table of Contents and circulate the list throughout the classroom. Each student should select one African American leader and write an essay about him or her. Students should take turns reading about their selection from the book.

Everyone should find two leaders in a magazine such as *Ebony, Jet, Essence* or *Black Enterprise* and make a collage for the entire class.

NOTES:

_____

_____

_____

_____

_____

_____

## The Journal:
Write who your favorite leader is and why.

## Postscript...
On your index cards tell the class what the person did to become well known and whether that person is living or dead.

## Materials: (HG)

- *Lessons From History*, Chapter 6
- Flags
- Poster Boards
- Crayons or Markers (red, black, and green)

## Procedure:

Read Chapter 6 in *Lessons From History* and discuss the various elements of Black Culture.

Working in your Harambee Group, create an African flag and make up a rap song about your culture.

NOTES:

_____

_____

_____

_____

_____

_____

_____

_____

_____

_____

_____

## The Journal:

List some of the things you like about your culture and why.

## Postscript...

Discuss the meaning of culture in *Lessons From History*. How is your culture distinctive in terms of food, religion, dialect, and holidays?

**Materials:**
- Paper
- Pen

**Procedure:**

Define and discuss the word "dialect".

Discuss some situations in which it is more acceptable to speak Standard English. In which situations are dialects more appropriate? Select someone to roleplay a job interview. The interviewee is to speak Black English and then Standard English. Roleplay the same situations as a talk show host. Write conversational sentences that are appropriate for each setting. Use the phrases to play the game "Is it Standard English or Black English?".

Use other dialects as well.

NOTES:

_____

_____

_____

_____

_____

**The Journal:**

In your journal, express yourself in some phrases using the Black English dialect and put the translations below them.

**Postscript...**

Identify situations in which Black English and other dialects are used on television, radio, in print media, and billboards.

## Materials:
- Pen
- Index Cards
- Poster Board
- Markers
- Paint
- Brushes
- Streamers

## Procedure:
Create your own speech about something that interests you. The speech should be two minutes in length. Use index cards to cue yourself as you speak. It might be helpful to make an outline of your material before you create your cards. If you would like to pretend you're a politician, make up your own posters and decorate with streamers.

NOTES:

_____

_____

_____

_____

_____

## The Journal:
Imagine you are making a speech and campaigning for public office. Record what state you might be in, what kind of audience it is and what you would like to talk about.

## Postscript...
View videotapes of effective speakers. Follow these guidelines that help them to be effective: maintain good eye contact, speak loudly and clearly, keep a good posture, have an interesting subject, and look around to keep audience's attention and ensure interest.

## Materials:
- Radio
- Music Tapes

## Procedure:
Listen to three songs and share with each other the message that the music has. Are these messages positive or negative? What is the general subject and how does the music make you feel?

Who are your favorite musical artists?

Jazz _____

_____

_____

Gospel _____

_____

_____

Rap_____

_____

_____

R & B _____

_____

_____

## The Journal:
Write down your favorite song and a letter to the artist telling him or her how much you enjoyed it.

## Postscript:
Create your own song. Share with the others what kind of song it is. Some music that African Americans created include: rap, jazz, and rhythm and blues. Does your song have a similar message to the ones you listen to on the radio?

## Materials:
✐ Pen
✐ Paper

## Procedure:
On a sheet of paper, record daily how much time you spend doing various activities and total the time spent.

Do you devote enough time to reach your goals or do you need to change your schedule?

Time is very precious and should always be used wisely. Based on your daily record, write down some of the things you will eliminate from your daily routine to help you spend your time more wisely.

NOTES:

_____

_____

_____

_____

_____

_____

_____

_____

## The Journal:
Record your favorite activity and also what you like to do the least.

## Postscript...
There are only 24 hours in a day. Are you getting enough rest? Do you finish everything you want to do? Being successful requires careful planning. Think about how you could make better use of your time.

**Materials: (HG)**
- TV
- Paper
- Pen

## Procedure:

Look at three 30 minute programs and two commercials. Write a report.

What are the shows about?

Were the characters good, evil, funny or sad?

What were they trying to sell in the commercials?

Did they show other things in the commercial besides the product, that attracted your attention?

If so, why do you think this was done?

Let's Talk About It:
Share your report with your Harambee Group. Each student should talk about why he or she believes everyone should be more selective about the television shows being watched.

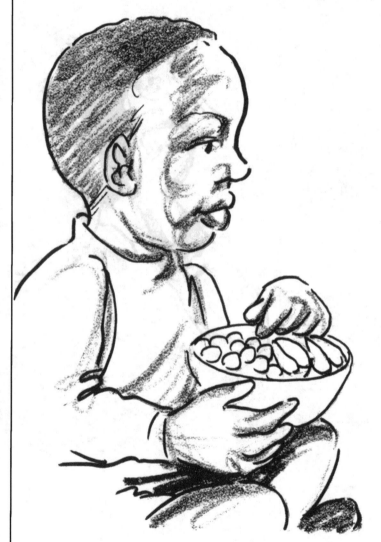

## The Journal:

Write down your favorite television program and how you would make it more interesting.

## Postscript...

Do you think violence should be on television? How do you feel about it? Write a letter to the producer of a television show explaining your views.

## Materials:
- Index Cards
- *Abdul and the Designer Tennis Shoes*

## Procedure:
A value is what we consider important in life. To some, family is important. To others, material items such as foreign cars, designer clothes, and expensive jewelry are major priorities.

As you read *Abdul*, think about some of the things that were important to the children in this book.
Look at the people around you and on television. What are the values that you see portrayed?
What is a value?
Why do we need values?

NOTES:

_____

_____

_____

_____

_____

_____

_____

BE A CHAMPION
"BUY DESIGNER
SHOES"

## The Journal:
Write down some of the things that are most important to you.

## Postscript...
Discuss the following items so that you can appreciate what you value, who you admire, what you like to buy, where you like to go, and your favorite pastimes.

## Materials:
- Pen
- Magazines
- Newspaper

## Procedure:
The purpose of advertising is to sell, sell, sell! Sometimes this can be in the form of a product, a service or an attempt to persuade someone's opinion.

Select three ads and try to explain what they are trying to sell. Are they trying to tell you extra things besides trying to get you to buy something?

Think about this: Do you need $100 shoes to play well?

_____

_____

What is the real purpose of footwear?

_____

_____

How important is it to wear designer clothes?

_____

_____

## The Journal:
Write down your favorite commercial-one that made you really want to buy something that was advertised.

# Advertising Images

## Postscript...
Discuss how advertisers try to influence your shopping decisions. Write your own commercial. What would you advertise and why?

## Materials:
✏ *I'm Special, Too*

## Procedure:
Discuss the importance of school in *I'm Special Too*. How is school meaningful in your life?

Write down your favorite subjects. _____

_____

Is it better to have a strict teacher or an easy teacher?

_____

What are the advantages and disadvantages of both?

_____

_____

_____

If you were to become a teacher when you grow up, would you want your students to be the type of student you are? Why or why not?

_____

_____

_____

## The Journal:
Write down what you like most about school, your favorite class and activity.

## Postscript...
Discuss how school has helped people attain their goals in life. Ask your parents what they believe is the purpose of school.

## Materials:

✐ Construction Paper
✐ Markers

## Procedure:

Use your Notes section to describe why you believe friends are important. Make a card for one of your friends to let them know they're appreciated.

NOTES

_____
_____
_____
_____
_____
_____
_____
_____
_____
_____
_____
_____
_____
_____

## The Journal:

Write down what you like best about your favorite friend.

## Postscript...

Discuss what friendship means and how your friends influence you.

## Materials: (HG)
- Kente cloth
- African fabric
- African crowns

## Procedure:
Working with your Harambee Group, create a Council of Elders to judge a case. The case should be a situation involving two people. It appears that one person convinced the other to do something dishonest and they both are trying to blame each other. The Council should question both parties and determine who is at fault. The Council should also find a positive way to help both persons avoid a similar occurrence in the future. The Council will wear kente cloth, African fabric and crowns.

NOTES:

_____

_____

_____

_____

_____

_____

_____

## The Journal:
Write down a situation where someone tried to talk you into doing something wrong and you resisted.

## Postscript...
Discuss why people try to convince others to do something wrong. Are they trying to get you into trouble? Are you afraid of being called a wimp or sissy for saying no? How can one overcome any fears?

## Materials:

- *Shining Legacy*, pp. 40-47
- Coloring Materials
- Any book on Kwanzaa
- Poster Board

## Procedure:

A value system consists of qualities and beliefs that are important to ourselves, our families, our communities, and our people. The Nguzo Saba is the African value system. It means seven principles in Kiswahili. To learn about these principles, read the pages of *Shining Legacy*.

Using the straw mat design (or other symbols of Kwanzaa), create a poster that lists all seven principles.

Let's Celebrate Kwanzaa!

Mkeka - straw mat
Kinara - candle holder
Mishumaa - seven candles
Muhindi - ears of corn
Zawadi - gifts
Mazao - fruit
Kikombe - unity cup

NOTES:

_____

_____

_____

## The Journal:
Write down what Kwanzaa means to you.

## Postscript...
Write down what Kwanzaa represents to you, your family, and friends. How can you put the principles into use? Discuss how the Nguzo Saba (seven principles) are cherished during Kwanzaa time?

# Kuumba Means Creativity

**Materials: (HG)**
- Paper
- Pen

## Procedure:

Kuumba is the 6th principle of the Nguzo Saba (seven principles). It means Creativity - to always do as much as we can in the way we can, in order to leave our community more beautiful and beneficial than when we inherited it.

Working with your Harambee Group, decide on a project to make your neighborhood a better, cleaner, and more attractive place to live.

NOTES:

_____

_____

_____

_____

_____

_____

_____

_____

_____

_____

## The Journal:
Write about something that you'd like to do for a project and plan for it.

## Postscript...
Attend a City Council Meeting, School Board Meeting, or Neighborhood Planning Committee and discuss how that group practices Kuumba.

**Materials: (HG)**
- Black Enterprise
- Neighborhood newspaper

Ujamaa - Cooperative Economics

Harambee
Time
#31

## Procedure:
UJAMAA (Cooperative Economics) is the 4th principle of the Nguzo Saba. Find examples of Cooperative Economics in a newspaper or magazine.

Can you think of any ways to apply this principle in your classroom?

Think of a business you could create with your Harambee Group. Ask your group these questions:

What product or service would you provide?

What skills and education must your employees have?

How much would you charge for your product or service?

What type of people could use your product or service?

Would you advertise?

What would you name the business?

Write down the responses and call it the Harambee Business Plan.

## The Journal:
Write down the type of business you might like to start one day.

## Postscript...
Visit a business owned by an African American and interview him/her. Find out how that person got started. How significant was education? Were there any other factors that contributed to his/her success? Maybe Ujamaa?

# Becoming a Man or Woman

**Materials:**
- 📖 *Herstory*, p. 1-9
- 📖 *Coming of Age*, p. 66-67

**Procedure:**
Read *Herstory* and *Coming of Age*. Select someone to be the moderator and discuss the signs of manhood, womanhood or both. How does one learn how to be a man or woman? Which of the following describes manhood/ womanhood?
Getting pregnant,
managing a house,
fighting,
studying,
working,
caring for others,
having well-developed hips and breasts,
growing a beard or moustache

NOTES:

_____

_____

_____

_____

_____

_____

_____

**The Journal:**
Write down how you would like your life to be once you become an adult.

**Postscript...**
Rites of Passage is a process through which boys and girls are trained to be men and women. Interview someone who has gone through this program. How can you organize your own?

AAI copyright 1992

45

# The SETCLAE Student Profile

## 6th Grade

## Instructions

Please answer the following questions on the answer sheet and think very hard about how you feel before answering each one. THERE ARE NO RIGHT OR WRONG ANSWERS. We want YOUR answers.

## Part I

Read each statement or question. If it is true for you, circle "a" on the answer sheet. If it is not true for you, circle "b". Answer every question, even if it's hard to decide. (Just think about yourself and what's important to you.) Select only one answer for each question.

| | | | |
|---|---|---|---|
| 1. | I like to be alone sometimes. | a. Yes | b. No |
| 2. | I enjoy public speaking. | a. Yes | b. No |
| 3. | Cleaning up should be done collectively. | a. Yes | b. No |
| 4. | School will help me to accomplish my own goals. | a. Yes | b. No |
| 5. | I enjoy looking for positive things to say about people. | a. Yes | b. No |
| 6. | I have personal goals. | a. Yes | b. No |
| 7. | I would rather do an extra credit project by myself than with a small group. | a. Yes | b. No |
| 8. | I get upset when things don't go my way. | a. Yes | b. No |
| 9. | School is boring most of the time. | a. Yes | b. No |
| 10. | I speak more than one dialect. | a. Yes | b. No |
| 11. | If I don't see a trash can, I throw my trash on the ground. | a. Yes | b. No |
| 12. | I like participating in special projects like science fairs and spelling bees. | a. Yes | b. No |
| 13. | When the truth is hard to say, I don't say it. | a. Yes | b. No |
| 14. | My friends are more important to me than my family. | a. Yes | b. No |
| 15. | My neighborhood is a good place to live in. | a. Yes | b. No |
| 16. | I can get any job I want, if I work at it hard enough. | a. Yes | b. No |
| 17. | I like being with people that are different from me. | a. Yes | b. No |
| 18. | I like me! | a. Yes | b. No |

| 19. | Do you believe you can have your own business when you get older? | a. Yes | b. No |
| 20. | The contribution I make to the world is not as important as the contributions of more famous people. | a. Yes | b. No |
| 21. | African Americans have not made many achievements in math, science, technology, and business. | a. Yes | b. No |
| 22. | If I could, I would make friends with people of all races. | a. Yes | b. No |
| 23. | Black people are not able to compete with others in many areas. | a. Yes | b. No |
| 24. | I want to be able to speak Standard English in certain situations. | a. Yes | b. No |

# Part II

Read each item carefully. If it is something that is important to you, circle "a" on the answer sheet. If it is not important to you (it doesn't really matter or has nothing to do with you), circle "b". Take your time and think about it. THERE ARE NO RIGHT OR WRONG ANSWERS. We want to know YOUR FEELINGS.

| 1. | Helping others | a. Important to me | b. Not important to me |
| 2. | What others think of me | a. Important to me | b. Not important to me |
| 3. | Reading in a study group | a. Important to me | b. Not important to me |
| 4. | Television as a way to receive most of my information | a. Important to me | b. Not important to me |
| 5. | Solving problems by fighting | a. Important to me | b. Not important to me |
| 6. | Learning about my family members - dead and living | a. Important to me | b. Not important to me |
| 7. | Working with others on short and long-term projects | a. Important to me | b. Not important to me |
| 8. | Doing whatever my friends do | a. Important to me | b. Not important to me |
| 9. | Wearing expensive clothes | a. Important to me | b. Not important to me |
| 10. | Doing well in school | a. Important to me | b. Not important to me |
| 11. | Speaking up for myself and my ideas | a. Important to me | b. Not important to me |
| 12. | Being positive most of the time | a. Important to me | b. Not important to me |
| 13. | Living conditions in Africa | a. Important to me | b. Not important to me |

## Part III

Read each statement carefully. Read the choices. Then select:

"a" if the statement accurately describes you and your feelings.

"b" if the statement does not accurately describe you and your feelings.

Circle them on the answer sheet.

If asked to describe my personality to someone I'd never met, I would use words like:

| | | | |
|---|---|---|---|
| 1. | a leader | a. Yes | b. No |
| 2. | confident | a. Yes | b. No |
| 3. | mature | a. Yes | b. No |
| 4. | critical of others | a. Yes | b. No |
| 5. | proud of my culture | a. Yes | b. No |
| 6. | easily bored | a. Yes | b. No |
| 7. | Africa is a dark continent filled with hunger, poverty and ignorance. | a. True | b. False |
| 8. | I can list five living African American men that are doing positive things in their family, business, church, community, or some other organization. | a. Yes | b. No |

List them below.

1) _____

2) _____

3) _____

4) _____

5) _____

9. Select the one that is most important to you.  Choose only one!

                       a. being popular          b. doing well in school

## Part IV

Read the following statements and choices for answers carefully. Then pick the answer that most accurately describes your feelings. Circle the letter in front of your answer on the answer sheet.

There are NO RIGHT OR WRONG ANSWERS.  Choose the answer that is right for YOU.

1.  When my friends have fun without me, I
    a.  am happy that they are having fun.
    b.  don't even think about it.
    c.  wish they weren't having fun without me.

2.  When I hear something negative about a person, I
    a.  can't wait to tell someone else.
    b.  talk to the person to see how I can help.
    c.  try to find out more, because it's interesting.

3.  When someone says something about me that is not good but is true, I
    a.  get upset.
    b.  don't want to be around them anymore.
    c.  listen and learn from their observations.

4.  When someone makes fun of me,
    a.  I get upset.
    b.  I am hurt.
    c.  I laugh with them.
    d.  I make a joke of it.
    e.  I don't like it.

5.  When I am talking to someone, most of the time I look
    a.  at their hands.
    b.  into their eyes.
    c.  at the floor.
    d.  all around.

6.  I always make sure I am neat and clean in my appearance.
    a.  never
    b.  once in a while
    c.  most of the time

7. Money is important for
    a. buying expensive clothes.
    b. building the community in which we live.
    c. buying whatever I want.
    d. saving for future plans.

8. A girl becomes a woman when (select the answer that is most important to you)
    a. she has a baby.
    b. her body becomes more developed (she has breasts and hair under her arms).
    c. she takes care of herself and her family.
    d. she can talk back to her mother.
    e. she has a boyfriend.

9. When I do poorly on my schoolwork, I
    a. don't really care.
    b. know I tried my best.
    c. know I should try harder.
    d. know it's only because I can't do any better.
    e. know the teacher gave us work that was too hard or boring.

10. In my involvement with organizations, I
    a. like to hold a leadership position.
    b. like to work as a team.
    c. don't like doing the dirty work.
    d. often disagree with other members.

11. When I need help, I
    a. get frustrated.
    b. ask for it.
    c. try to figure it out myself.

12. I pick my friends because
    a. they look good.
    b. they are cool.
    c. they are understanding.
    d. they have something to offer me.

13. I am glad I am the race I am.
    a. Yes
    b. No

14. I chose the answer above because
    a. I am proud of my heritage.
    b. I should be glad.
    c. I study my history and culture.
    d. my friends say it's important.

15. I like my favorite music because
    a. of its rhythm for dancing.
    b. of its positive messages.
    c. of its ability to help me relax.
    d. the rappers curse and insult women.
    e. the videos are nice.

16. A boy becomes a man when
    a. he can handle drugs and crime.
    b. he makes a baby.
    c. he takes responsibility for his actions.
    d. he can fight well.

17. When I attend assemblies or special events, I like to sit
    a. in the middle of the auditorium.
    b. in the front of the auditorium.
    c. in the back of the auditorium.

18. When I set a goal, I
    a. expect someone to make it happen for me.
    b. plan how I will do it and make the first step.
    c. just think about it very hard.
    d. ask my friends to get me started.

19. When the teacher leaves the room, I
    a. talk.
    b. stop doing my work.
    c. look at who is being disobedient.
    d. find something quiet to do once I finish my work.

20. Learning about one's culture and heritage is very important and helps me feel good about who I am.
    a. Yes
    b. No

21. I like my favorite television program because
    a. it's very funny.
    b. I enjoy the action.
    c. I enjoy the "scenery" (cars, clothes, houses, etc.).
    d. it is educational.
    e. it makes me think and discuss important issues with others.

22. I am beautiful or handsome because I have
    a. light skin.
    b. dark skin.
    c. natural hair.
    d. long hair.
    e. a thin shape.

23. Answering these questions was
    a. very enjoyable.
    b. no big deal.
    c. a good way to take a closer look at my personal development.

24. Africa has many cities.
    a. True          b. False

25. Africa is the Motherland of Black people all over the world.
    a. True          b. False

26. Egypt, also known as Kemet (which means Land of the Blacks), is in Africa which is the cradle of civilization.
    a. True          b. False

27. African people have always resisted domination all over the world.
    a. True          b. False

28. Africa is mostly jungle.
    a. True          b. False

29. Tarzan movies show you what Africa is like and used to be like.
    a. True          b. False

30. Africa is a continent on which there is a cultural unity more important than the differences we hear about in the news.
    a. True          b. False

Using the definitions on the right, choose the letter that you feel best describes each of the seven principles listed (Nguzo Saba).

___ 31. UMOJA            a. to build our stores and businesses and profit from them together.

___ 32. KUJICHAGULIA   b. to have a collective goal of building and developing our community.

___ 33. UJIMA            c. to always be creative in the ways we improve our communities.

___ 34. UJAMAA          d. being determined to speak up for ourselves.

___ 35. NIA              e. to work on challenges together and feel responsible as a group.

___ 36. KUUMBA         f. to believe in ourselves that we will do great things.

___ 37. IMANI             g. to keep in touch with and offer support to friends, neighbors, and community.

# SOMETHING YOU SHOULD KNOW.......

## Group # 2 - African Countries

**Nigeria** - This West African country is Africa's most populated country. It is rich with oil.

**Kenya** - This beautiful East African country is home for the Gikuyu community. Jomo Kenyatta led them to freedom.

**Egypt** - Civilization began here. It is home of the great pyramids, temples, tombs and King Tut.

**Azania** - Sometimes called South Africa, it is a country filled with gold and diamonds. We all must remove apartheid, a form of slavery. Azania is the home of Nelson Mandela.

**Tanzania** - It is an East African country and home of the great former President Julius Nyerere.


## Group # 3 - African Communities

**Ashanti** - A community from Ghana. Many residents work as weavers of beautiful kente cloth and carvers of the Ashanti stool for the king.

**Chagga** - A community where the children play among others the same age and are taught to be adults by the time they are 15 years old.

**Pondo** - A community where the children learn self-defense at an early age.

**Fanti** - A community in West Africa. They pour libation which is pouring a little wine on the ground to honor their dead family members (ancestors).

**Ikoma** - A community in West Africa. They gather honey to eat and sell.


## Group # 4 - Black Colleges

**Morehouse College** - An all-male school in Atlanta, Georgia. Martin Luther King, Jr. and Spike Lee graduated from Morehouse.

**Hampton University** - A college in Hampton, Virginia with 4500 students. They have their own radio and TV stations.

**Spelman College** -An all-female school with nearly 200 students. It's right next door to Morehouse College. Bill and Camille Cosby gave the school $20 million dollars in 1988.

**Tuskegee Institute** - Founded by Booker T. Washington. They have a pre-veterinarian program (animal doctors). It's in Tuskegee, Alabama.

**Howard University** - One of the largest Black colleges in the country. It's in Washington, D.C. and has its own medical school.

# SETCLAE PRONUNCIATION GLOSSARY

## Kiswahili

Phonics

a - short a    i - long e

e - long a    o - long o

u - long u

| | |
|---|---|
| Jambo - Hello | Mzee - Elder |
| Habari Gani - What is the News? | Chakula - Food |
| Njema - Fine | Choo - Toilet |
| Asante - Thank you | Hodi hodi - Hurry |
| Asante Sana - Thank you very much | Tutaonana - Goodbye |
| Mama - Mother | Moja - One |
| Baba - Father | Mbili - Two |
| Ndada - Sister | Tatu - Three |
| Ndugu - Brother | Nne - Four |
| Watoto - Children | Tano - Five |
| Mtoto - Child | Sita - Six |
| Mwalimu - Teacher | Saba - Seven |
| Mwanafunzi - Student | Nane - Eight |
| Shule - School | Tisa - Nine |
| Yebo - Yes | Kumi - Ten |
| La - No | Umoja - Unity |
| Acha - Stop | Nisamehe - Excuse me |
| Kujichagulia-Self-determination | Tafadali - Please |
| Ujima - Collective work & responsibility | Mzuri - Good |
| Ujamaa - Cooperative economics | Nia - Purpose |
| Harambee - Let's pull together | Imani - Faith |
| Pamoja Tutashinda - Together we will win | Kuumba - Creativity |